Queer Hagiographies

Queer Hagiographies

Audra Puchalski

Finalist for the Charlotte Mew Prize

HEADMISTRESS PRESS

ISBN 978-1-7335345-5-0

Cover art © 2016 by C. Finley. SANTA LUCIA The Channel of Inspiration (Full Bed). 74x54in acrylic on canvas.

Cover & book design by Mary Meriam.

PUBLISHER
Headmistress Press
60 Shipview Lane
Sequim, WA 98382
Telephone: 917-428-8312
Email: headmistresspress@gmail.com
Website: headmistresspress.blogspot.com

CONTENTS

Saint Hilda

A serpent eats another serpent and then
regurgitates the other serpent, her jaw
unhinged, her mouth a chalice.
A bird dives to the surface of the lake,
swoops up: swoop as antidote to dive, regurgitate
as antidote to eat, antidote as antidote
to venom, the venom of the serpent, willful length
of muscle, fanged hunger traversing the earth
looking for something to swallow. The snake
of thought and the snake of imagination
eat each other and regurgitate each other over
and over forever, unless you turn them both
to stone. It's easy. My throat fills up
like a balloon, fills with venom
and the curse spills down my chin, dirty water
from a flooded gutter. At home, we say
our rosaries—our fingers burnish
the small device of our faith, guide to how
many times we're permitted to hail, hail Mary
together, famished, feral, humid with
prayer until we crumble like stones
raked up in the garden that turn out
to be clumps of earth. Two
unlocked doors, handsome arm
wrapped in mine, her arm like strong branches
when as a child I would lift my body up
branch by warm-skinned branch past heaven and on
beyond to some other place, a place unlocked—
an open door opening on openness, a sky with no top
no floor but a sheer scrim of shimmering vapor,
a single bird that disappears. The wool of her sleeve.
The smell of fruit coming from nowhere.
The smallest drops of salt. Sun-warmed tree,
for you I turn serpents to stone. Clump

of dirt that crumbles at a touch, for you
I turn serpents to stone. Rosary bead
rubbed to a gleam by our hot fingers,
for you I turn thriving muscle to cold fossil,
roving ribbon of desire to deathless spiral.

Saint Rita

You knife my heart, you tempered
bright thing my flesh breaks for.
You know my every throb,
you drain my blood, you want
an explanation. You abandon me,
you won't leave. You commit
to me—me, a moth
pinned to paper. You,
the pin. You, my roof
caving in. My sunset and I'm
stranded. My kitten, piercing
my skin with your thin
white claws. Leash, jerking me
back, knocking the wind
out of me. Breath, blowing
out my last candle.
And me, your diamond-studded
thousand-pound collar:
I sparkle even harder in the dark.

Saint Eulalia

A ribbon stuffed inside my mouth,
bursting out in wet curls the moment I open it:
Fuck your gods! I'm going live. I'm snapchatting this
to the whole school. I'm @ing all your faves. So yeah,
strip me. Strap me to a broken door and make me swallow
smoke, pervs. That door just keeps on opening!
I just keep stepping through it! I slip right through like soup
through the tines of your fork as you starve. Slip like water
down your throat into your lungs as you drown.
Try to expose me and a hull of dust and vapor winds
around me, a blanket of snow enfolds me. Try and pull on me, try
and pick at me, try and bury me somewhere I won't
keep laughing in your speechless faces! I eat your rage.
Your shame tastes sweet in my mouth, warm
as fresh blood in my heart, warm as my blood running
down this plank as *fuck your gods!* unfurls in damp ripples. Water
pursues your doom and my salvation, water fills
my mouth, water surrounds, water fogs up your glasses,
obscures your creepy stares, water makes a blind maze
of your life, water makes you grope like the sick gropers
you are and I'm laughing all the way to the grave! Hardly
a martyrdom, this comic ecstasy. Hardly suffering, your weak
thrusts of the knife. A dove asleep in my mouth,
bursting forth wet-feathered: *fuck your gods.* Decked out
in my fog-white dress—it's couture, assholes. It's designer
and you're not my dad. You wouldn't get it. I'm dripping
in exquisite vapor, in princess-cut ice crystals. I'm a goddamn
treasure chest of sanctity! I'm bleeding holiness down this
filthy slab. This fire is cooled by my perfect body, this smoke
is purified inside my gorgeous lungs. I'm riding white horses
in paradise. I'm the closest thing to God you'll never see.

Saint Alban

I thought I couldn't be a person until a man
hurt my feelings but he never did,
hair flip. I definitely do not want pain,
don't even wanna shiver, evenings
without my jacket, triceps
twitching holding my body back
from sensation like a gravel road and me
about to faceplant in gravel, my bones
already gravel, crushed—not
by a man—the soft flesh fled or flayed
open and shattering exposed, radiant
and I am dazzled, licking the pebbles,
mist in my mouth and once again carrying my
leathering disembodied head to my grave
because I'm helpful like that. *Go ahead,*
I said, or *yes please, cut off my head,*
I have a weird feeling I'll kinda like it, I said,
stupid. Walking the labyrinth of the hillside,
carrying my own head, entering this
hillside in my index of the numerous hillsides
where I have carried my own head helpfully
to my grave, the nostrils flared with the sharp
intake of breath, the throat stretching open—
the labyrinth of passages inside the head
can be distracting if you're not sure where
you're headed and I'm not. Which way to my
grave today? Anatomy, index, skinbound
book, folds in the brain, forget what I don't
want, sinuses, forget the location
of my grave, synapse, forget the rosebush tangled
in my path, uvula, forget the drudgery of
these verdant hillsides, drudgery especially
severe combined with the depressing cargo
of my body and yeah when I think about it
my head too, the whole thing complaining
every step and nowhere to get rid of it.

Saint Francis Xavier

"I shall never forget you. Entirely your own—Ignatius"
– Saint Ignatius, in a letter to Saint Francis Xavier

Holy these scapulae, this ache in buried
muscle strung taut to femur. Holy this flank
thwacked by your blesséd hand soft
as peony, hand that justifies.
Holy the wet grass in unceasing
rain and holy the unceasing rain
of winter turning this half-desert green.
To hold your hand, to graze
the bundled petals with my fingertips,
to test the blossom's density in my palm. Holy
this heap of letters, holy each scrap,
each caught breath, this trail
of breadcrumbs stretching two directions
into darkness. Holy the place
we sit. Holy the thirty holy seconds I stop
grasping at you and let you have me.

Saint Ignatius

As I voyage across the continent, I write the wild beasts
who will devour me when I arrive in Rome.
Dear beasts who are to devour me, I write, *I cannot wait*

*for you to devour me. Too long I've been half-devoured
by desire—you, wild beasts, must finish me, disheveled
plate of leftovers, before I go cold and crust over.*

*Unfurl my twisted organs, swallow my broken heart
and let it reunite dissovled inside you, shred
the porous membrane between me and erasure, me*

*and forever, me and freedom. May nothing else
entice me. May my darkest parts be brought to light.
I crave his blood—I mean my blood—I mean your claws.*

*If they hold me back from you, my bones will ache
with wanting to be ground between your teeth. Partake
of me catholically. Let me thrill when you pounce on me,*

*not your prey but your beneficiary. Not my killers but
my saviors. This world has always spat me out—
I know you won't. This world has refused me—now*

*I cast it aside, leaping joyfully into your open jaws,
a lover reunited with his beloved. I stalk
toward you, escorted by soldiers and angels,*

feeling you draw near, ready for my marriage vows.

Saint Isidore

1

Bundle of dry grass. Airborne spear. I
am seeded, sweetening, a crosswise

leaf. Hello, I am
                    a simple farmer. I am

relishing the danger of it. Scorched,
crenellated, burned to the bottom

of a cast iron pan.
                    I am a lamb, a lamb

in a wedge of hay, rinsed and cultivated,
raw and molding, covered, wild fungus,

thinly sliced,
                a perfect swirl of wool.

2

The danger is in the crosswise flourish,
the sweet molding within the fungus.
The danger is in the wild, in the slice,
in the scorch of it. The danger is,

what if this bundle
                              unravels? The danger

is in rinsing the lamb. There's danger
in relishing excessively. The danger
consists of: seed, spear, harvest, scythe.
The danger is the lamb may cry. The danger is

you might relish
                              the crying. The danger is

if no lambs are born, or just one lamb but
it dies. The danger is losing your footing
in the thick swirl of grain and falling slowly
down the airless silo. The danger is wedged
between the barn door and the barrel.
The danger is that cultivation is a cover

for something coarse
                              and raw, blood soaking

through the thin leaves of the almanac.

3

The only spring lamb is dead, molding
atop a wedge of hay, blood soaking through
the thin leaves of the almanac, perfect swirls
of wool. The raw crops, ready for harvest,
for the swallow, ready to be bundled and rinsed.

Let me recultivate a relish
                                  for catastrophe.

Let me endanger innocent vegetation. Let me
scorch the surface of the field with the pure heat
of truth. A single spear of asparagus slices

the darkness, sweetening,
                                  coarsening, interrupting

layers of soil, rewilding
                                  the field, unclaiming

the field, I sit back and watch each thing
unravel, be swallowed, go completely to seed.

As though seed were
                                  a place, as though seed

were a problem. Watch the heap of our efforts
drift like dust off the edge of the earth. Let it die

and if it won't die,
                                  go out there and kill it.

Saint Jude

His right hand
on my shoulder blade and following's
like falling: effortless, irresistible,   his body

a steeple drawing my eye from as far
as I could run.   His mouth alongside
      my ear, my body a stalk dead
      winter-long, now drawing
      life from the thawing
      earth on the first
      day of spring, xylem full of   his blood.
Disciple to his desire
      disciplined to his wishes   his breath
      a fog on the glass of my mind   his sigh

a rainbow sketched across the nimbus of my life
a sudden gesture in stillness.   His body a vault
      where I secure my weakness.   His body resonant
as the skirt of the bell in the steeple and   his body the steeple
      visible from everywhere.   His threat. His embrace.

Immersed in a sea, bound to my body
      afloat in the current of   his attention.
Frost evaporates. The ice on my skin
turns to sweat. My rags disintegrate,
unpeel at the seams, drenched in   his body,
his blood, his voice,   his mouth.

Saint Marciana

Feathers, I say to the leopard. Fronds, to the bull.
A child peels open a flowerbud, rips it to pieces.
The bull's horns smell of jasmine, of ambrosia. My body
ambrosia-drenched as Diana smashed in the temple, her bloodless corpse
dismembered. Relieve me of it—leave me as shattered,
as virgin-martyred. If I could be stone. If I could be shattered.
Turned divine, easy as the meter turning 9s to 0s.
The tremor inside the fruit before the gush of nectar and the teeth.
The spark, the wick, the lantern hung at the end of the dark
tunnel of the way out of the unsurvivable. At the base
of the throat of the leopard. At the tip of the horns of the bull.
Feathers, shed without consequence. Fronds, falling away as they must.
Diana, virgin, spinster, dyke with her pack of dogs.
We destroy each other—feathers, to the leopard. Fronds,
to the bull. The tectonic swerve of my body toward
the piecemeal shifting of landscapes tearing themselves open,
clotting, the wound oozing latex, green skin re-growing over.
The earth turns toward what needs to be faced.
I uncurl like a fiddlehead, unfold like a bud,
tear myself open like a child an unopened flower,
robbing himself of the bloom, but the rosebush laughs
and blooms harder. Pluck me, prune me, tear me to pieces,
seed the earth with me. Feathers. Fronds. Blossoms. The leopard
is hungry. The temple virgins crouch around her.
The cauldron of the arena fills with blood.

Saint Catherine

The women collapse in unison because we are team players.
We breathe and turn our bodies toward the presumed sky
beyond the dark ceiling, our fingers spread like fronds

unfurling, a ring wrapped around a finger like a long hair,
clinging. Possible hells: one. Masses of hair in my mouth,

pulling out more and more, I choke on it.
Two. I am a vine in the rainforest. I climb
and climb towards the canopy, eyeless,
mindless. I never find the sun and die
without opening my single glorious bloom. Three.
Running up a spiral staircase in a doorless stairwell,
a tower extending forever in both directions,
and there's no one, not even a monster
to kill me—just stone and iron,
eternity and me. Four. I am being chased
by men and I use my wooden spoon to fling
dust and sticks in their faces. Five.
My eggs grow inside my body.
On their birthday, they burst out,
tear me apart, and devour me.

Without idleness I faint like a maidenhair fern.
I don't know how anyone can survive in this world.

Saint Lawrence

"I'm well done on this side. Turn me over!"
> – Saint Lawrence, patron saint of cooks and comedians,
> whilst being tortured on a hot gridiron

I walk around, sharp object
in hand, unable to not imagine it
plunging into my abdomen—
a martyrdom. Or
I switch on the burner and see
my hand slammed down
on the hot coil, and a kind of
relief. I am the prefect
who tortures me

and I am the mom
who hassles tirelessly
the child of me: not to touch,
to hold the knife point down,
to pull up my tights.

So all winter
in Michigan,
I picked my way down
treacherous frozen sidewalks,
my wool tights
webbed slightly
beneath my crotch
like the toes of an amphibian
evolved for speed through water.
My skirt fell
around my thighs,
a veil to obscure
my deformity. At any moment
I was ready to swim

rapidly away,
to propel myself
down the Huron River
through Ypsilanti
and Flat Rock,
to the Detroit River,
down the length
of Lake Erie
and Lake Ontario,
to follow the Saint Lawrence River
into Lake Saint Lawrence
and more Saint Lawrence River,
down the Canal de Beauharnois
into Lac Saint Louis,
more Saint Lawrence River
and then Lac-Saint-Pierre,
more Saint Lawrence River
and then the Gulf of Saint Lawrence
and then the Atlantic
to live out my days roving
the oceans,
a great monstrous
humanoid woolfish
of the sea.

Saint Julian of Norwich

Suffering, faithful, a dour parade
of visitors trundles past
my tiny window, asking
for help. I can't help.
An angelfish in a bishop hat,
a fossilized crustacean with a monocle,
a helmeted bacterium from outer space
can't help anyone. All I can do is talk
to God. And God says: dress in thorns
because your mother suffered; because
her book of pressed flowers
was lost in the fire; because
you are helpless and need mercy.
God says: descend, and in those
sodden passageways lick
what salt you may find. All is not
well. But shall it be? Let's hope.

Saint Emily

The juices drip from her hands. She won't fit in mine
no matter how wide I spread my fingers.
        I've been to the harbor
        and hated it. Why does
everyone sexualize Emily Dickinson?
Including me? Can't a woman just not have sex
        without anyone
        bothering her? Or,
we don't know she didn't, but there I go
again. I've been to the harbor and hated
        to see the boats
        chained in their slips.
How tenderly they acquiesce, how a soft touch
brings a giant to her dock. I wish I could be
        so easily moved
        by a gentle hand.
        She puts hers
        into my mouth.

Queer Hagiography

after Garth Nix and Kimiko Hahn

At the root of my queerness
at my queer root
a long black thread connects the necromancer to the spirit they control.
Or in real life
the dead tie their long black threads to us on their way out the door
so they can puppet us from the afterlife
from the grave
from the ocean where we tried to scatter them
from the parties where they hang out now
strewn with satin sheets, throw pillows, ruffles. Meanwhile
in Life, I hurl my body towards the earth
and by earth I mean your bones.
I press my bones against your bones without knowing why
even though the why is obvious
or I radiate my soft tissues and achy teeth with howling
for the same reason. I enter the garden,
touch its tulips cupping their dangerous pollen.
I pronoun them—
their sexuality volute and languid.
I adore the pines, the stand of them,
their erotic silence. I don't remember
choosing or writing the word "compelled."
A long black thread.
Gelatinous pearl of half-frozen water on the leaf of my bones' love for
the earth/you/death. A gully sopping with runoff,
brackish with minerals rising from mud—
that's my heart, that's my body when your bones come close
with their plantlike growths reaching towards the scant
light of the canopy. You rose. You pined,
needle-strewn as the forest floor. You hedged.

Genesis 1

In the beginning, there was a fly. There was a truck on a faraway highway. There was a fluffy blanket. Pretty much everything was already there, which was very convenient for God, who didn't really feel like doing anything that day. So she took a break. This is self care, she thought. But soon she was overcome by guilt and shame. I'm supposed to be the creator, I shouldn't be laying around doing nothing! So she lit the blanket on fire. She chased the fly around with a giant roll of newspaper and squashed it. She drove the truck off the road.

ABOUT THE AUTHOR

Audra Puchalski is from Michigan. She earned her MFA from the University of Michigan, where she won a Hopwood Award in Graduate Poetry. Her work has appeared in *Bat City Review, Juked, Salt Hill, The Rupture, Cutbank Online*, and elsewhere. She currently lives in Oakland, California.

ACKNOWLEDGMENTS

Many thanks to the editors of the following publications, in which these poems appeared, sometimes in earlier versions:

Juked: "Saint Lawrence" and "Saint Alban"

Bat City Review: "Saint Isidore"

Cotton Xenomorph: "Saint Ignatius"

Reservoir: "Saint Hilda"

Thank you to everyone who helped make these poems happen, namely Jane Cope, Pamela Stacey, Hannah Ensor, Gala Mukomolova, Gina Brandolino, Violet Ace Harlo, Sara Jane Stoner, and my love, aeryne james.

HEADMISTRESS PRESS BOOKS

Tender Age - Luiza Flynn-Goodlett

Low-water's Edge - Jean A. Kingsley

Routine Bloodwork - Colleen McKee

Queer Hagiographies - Audra Puchalski

Why I Never Finished My Dissertation - Laura Foley

The Princess of Pain - Carolyn Gage & Sudie Rakusin

Seed - Janice Gould

Riding with Anne Sexton - Jen Rouse

Spoiled Meat - Nicole Santalucia

Cake - Jen Rouse

The Salt and the Song - Virginia Petrucci

mad girl's crush tweet - summer jade leavitt

Saturn coming out of its Retrograde - Briana Roldan

i am this girl - gina marie bernard

Week/End - Sarah Duncan

My Girl's Green Jacket - Mary Meriam

Nuts in Nutland - Mary Meriam & Hannah Barrett

Lovely - Lesléa Newman

Teeth & Teeth - Robin Reagler

How Distant the City - Freesia McKee

Shopgirls - Marissa Higgins

Riddle - Diane Fortney

When She Woke She Was an Open Field - Hilary Brown

A Crown of Violets - Renée Vivien tr. Samantha Pious

Fireworks in the Graveyard - Joy Ladin

Social Dance - Carolyn Boll

The Force of Gratitude - Janice Gould

Spine - Sarah Caulfield

I Wore the Only Garden I've Ever Grown - Kathryn Leland

Diatribe from the Library - Farrell Greenwald Brenner

Blind Girl Grunt - Constance Merritt

Acid and Tender - Jen Rouse

Beautiful Machinery - Wendy DeGroat

Odd Mercy - Gail Thomas

The Great Scissor Hunt - Jessica K. Hylton

A Bracelet of Honeybees - Lynn Strongin

Whirlwind @ Lesbos - Risa Denenberg

The Body's Alphabet - Ann Tweedy

First name Barbie last name Doll - Maureen Bocka

Heaven to Me - Abe Louise Young

Sticky - Carter Steinmann

Tiger Laughs When You Push - Ruth Lehrer

Night Ringing - Laura Foley

Paper Cranes - Dinah Dietrich

On Loving a Saudi Girl - Carina Yun

The Burn Poems - Lynn Strongin

I Carry My Mother - Lesléa Newman

Distant Music - Joan Annsfire

The Awful Suicidal Swans - Flower Conroy

Joy Street - Laura Foley

Chiaroscuro Kisses - G.L. Morrison

The Lillian Trilogy - Mary Meriam

Lady of the Moon - Amy Lowell, Lillian Faderman, Mary Meriam

Irresistible Sonnets - ed. Mary Meriam

Lavender Review - ed. Mary Meriam